What happened long ago

Bible Stories retold by
Jean and Jennifer Rees
and Mary Batchelor

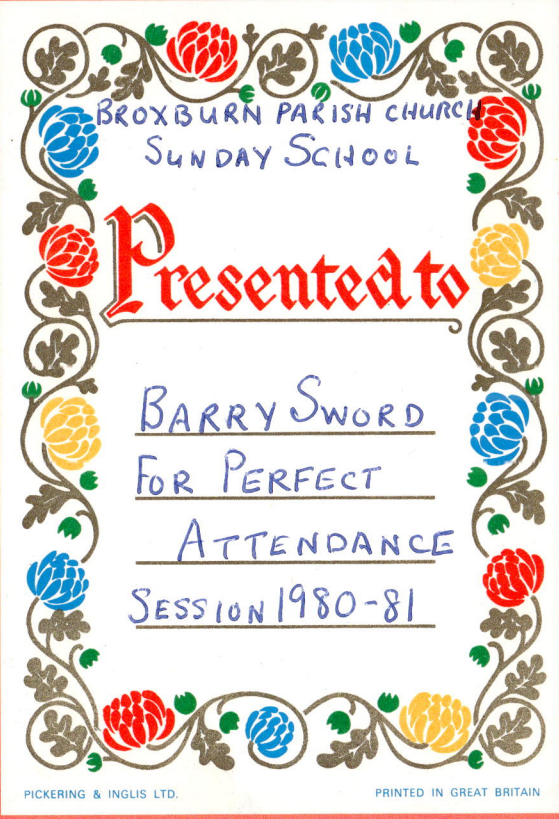

BROXBURN PARISH CHURCH
SUNDAY SCHOOL

Presented to

BARRY SWORD
FOR PERFECT
ATTENDANCE
SESSION 1980-81

PICKERING & INGLIS LTD.   PRINTED IN GREAT BRITAIN

Pickering & Inglis
LONDON · GLASGOW

ISBN 0 7208 2286 6
Cat. No. 11/4203

Printed in Great Britain

-NOEL SYERS-

The Man who made Everyone Laugh

God felt very sorry that He had put men on His beautiful earth, for they had all become horrid and unkind and there was only one person who still loved God. This man's name was Noah.

One day God said to him, "Noah, I am soon going to send a great flood of water to wash away all these wicked people, but I want you and your family to be safe. You are to build a great boat for you and your family, and some of every kind of animal, bird and insect."

Then God told Noah exactly how the ark (which was what the big boat was called) was to be built, and Noah went off to do it, even though it was an almost impossible thing. Nowadays it would take many men with great cranes a long time to build a boat as big as the ark was, and Noah and his sons had no proper tools, and only wooden pegs for nails.

Soon all the people round about were talking about Noah. "He's building a great big boat miles and miles away from the sea!" they said.

Then they came and laughed at him, and Noah would say to them sadly, "God is going to send a great flood to drown you, unless you are sorry for the wicked things you do."

At this, the people would laugh all the more, and say, "Poor Noah, he has gone quite mad."

Years passed and the ark was finished. The people still came from miles around to see this wonderful boat. It was three storeys high, and covered all over with oily pitch, to keep the water out.

Then God spoke again to Noah, "I want you to get two of every kind of animal to go into the ark. Then you and your family are to go in also. Take plenty of food with you, for in seven days time I will send the great flood." Once again Noah did as he was told, and when they were all safely inside God shut the door.

Then the people laughed as never before. "Poor Noah," they laughed, "shut up in a boat with all those smelly animals, and no water in sight!"

Then one of them felt something on his arm. It was a raindrop. Soon the rain was falling steadily. And it kept falling.

"Whatever can be happening?" they all cried as they began to get wet. "We had better run into our houses." But soon the flood waters began to come through their windows and doors. Some of them waded to the ark and pleaded to be let in, but the door was tight shut. It was too late.

"We must go to the tops of the mountains," they shouted. But soon even these were covered, and all the wicked people were never seen again.

The rain kept coming down for forty days. When it stopped, Noah opened one of the portholes in the ark and sent out a raven. It flew away and never came back.

After some time Noah wondered if there was any dry land, so he sent out a dove. The dove could not find anywhere to perch and so returned to the ark.

Seven days later Noah let the dove fly off again. That same evening it flew back, and what do you think it had in its beak? It was the leaf of an olive tree. Noah knew now that the water was going down, and that it would not be long before the flood had gone away altogether.

After another seven days, Noah let the dove fly out yet again. This time it did not come back, and Noah knew it must have found some place to rest.

Suddenly there was a horrible bump. The boat had landed safely on dry land. The door of the boat was opened, and out came all the animals with Noah and his family, because now there was food enough for them all.

As they all stood on top of the mountain a rainbow appeared. As they watched it in amazement, God spoke to them. "This is my rainbow," He said, "and whenever you see it, remember that I promise never again to send such a terrible flood on the earth."

And as they watched it fade, they knew that God would never break that promise.

Genesis 6:14-8:19

The King who disobeyed God

When Moses went to King Pharaoh with God's message that he had to set the people of Israel free, he was glad he was not alone because Pharaoh was furious. He sat on his great throne and glared at Moses. "Let all my useful slaves go," he shouted, "just because your God tells me to! Why should I? I don't even believe in Him."

"You must let the people go," answered Moses, "God will make you."

"He can't make me do anything," snarled Pharaoh. That same day Pharaoh ordered the people to work even harder, and, leaning back in his throne, he smiled, thinking how clever he was.

The people of Israel complained that they were being made to work too hard. But Pharaoh shouted at them, "You're lazy, get back to your work!" Then the people turned to Moses and Aaron. "It's because of you", they said bitterly, "that we are worse off."

Moses and Aaron became very unhappy. Moses spoke to God. "O God, why did you send me? Since I came, things have become worse." But God promised Moses, "Tell the people of Israel that I will set them free. Go back to Pharaoh, tell him to

-NOEL SYERS-

let My people go."

Moses met Pharaoh. "If you do not let the people go," he said, "God will turn all the water in Egypt into blood."

And that was what happened. "There is nothing for us to drink," cried the Egyptians, "and we cannot wash or cook."

"Call Moses," ordered Pharaoh grimly.

"If you will ask your God to change back our water," he promised, "I will set the slaves free."

But when God did, Pharaoh broke his promise. So God sent another plague. Thousands of frogs appeared all over Egypt. They hopped into their houses, their food and into their beds. There were frogs everywhere. Again Pharaoh promised to let the people go if Moses would get rid of the frogs. But once they had gone he changed his mind.

After that, so many terrible plagues were sent that the people of Egypt hardly knew what would happen next, and they went to Pharaoh and pleaded with him to let the slaves go.

"We are desperate," they said, "we have been bitten by lice, stung by flies, frightened by darkness, and covered with boils. Our cows are dead and locusts have eaten our food. It would be better to lose the slaves than to suffer this."

But Pharaoh was too proud to do as God told him.

Exodus 5:1-11:10

The Youngest of the Family

"If only I were braver," thought Gideon as he sat in his secret hideout. He was the youngest of the family, and loved to listen to the old men telling the stories of the days when God led the people through the dangerous wilderness, until He had brought them to this beautiful land, where the people had promised to serve Him.

"We did not keep our promise for long," thought Gideon sadly. "Most people have forgotten God. I suppose that is why the Midianites have come. God said that troubles would come if we broke our promise."

He shivered as he thought of the terrible enemy who came riding down on their fast running camels, burning the crops and killing everything in sight.

One day an angel visited Gideon. "YOU are going to lead an army to fight these Midianites," said the angel, "and you will win, because God will be with you."

In vain Gideon tried to explain that he was the youngest of the family, neither brave nor clever.

"God will help you," said the angel.

How God changed him! For soon he was the leader of the army of Israel. Most men had given up worshipping Baal and were ready to follow Gideon into battle against the Midianites.

Thirty-two thousand men had come to join the army when Gideon blew the trumpet to summon them. They were all very enthusiastic at first, but after a few days many of them secretly wished they hadn't offered to fight. How surprised they were when Gideon stood up and shouted—

"Attention! Any man who is afraid—let him go home."

Do you know how many crept away hoping no one would notice? Twenty-two thousand! Only ten thousand were left, but what a fine crowd of men.

Even this was too many, for God wanted everyone to know that they could win, only because they were trusting God.

Then God told Gideon to take the ten thousand soldiers down to the river and get them to drink. Those who curved the palms of their hands and brought the water up to their mouths, were to remain in the army, and those who knelt down and put their mouths in the water were sent home. After this further test, Gideon was left with only three hundred men!

Gideon gathered his men round him—"Listen to this plan that God has given me," he whispered. The tiny army could hardly believe their ears as they listened.

"If I did not know that God is with our leader, I would never take a risk like this," whispered one soldier. "Here we are going to fight the mighty Midianites with only a handful of men, and not a sword amongst us."

"Be quiet," hissed his friend, "just do as Gideon told us."

"Well," muttered the other, "I've never gone into battle with a water jar, a fire torch and a trumpet before."

"Don't forget," said his friend, "when Gideon gives the signal, blow your trumpet, break your jar, wave the fire brand and shout."

The Midianites slept restlessly. As they tossed and turned, suddenly the silence of the night was shattered by what to them sounded like thousands of trumpets. As they sprang from their tents, Gideon's men broke their jars, and the weird light from their torches flared up all round the terrified Midianites.

"We are surrounded by many armies," they screamed, and began to rush madly here and there. In the darkness, each man thought his friends were enemy soldiers, so they began to kill one another, and as the shouts and strange lights drew nearer they ran for their lives, never to return.

Judges 6-7:22

The Long Haired Soldier

One day Samson was walking through the enemy's cornfields.

"It will soon be harvest time," he thought, "and the Philistines will cut this corn. Now if only I could spoil it they would be so hungry we would defeat them."

Then he had this clever plan. He collected three hundred foxes and tied torches to their tails. This made the foxes run with fear through the cornfields, and soon the whole countryside was on fire. Samson killed many enemy soldiers, then hid himself.

How angry the Philistines were! "We must catch this Samson," they said to the Israelites "Find Samson, or we will kill you."

Then they sat down to plan how they would kill Samson when he came. They were soon shouting with excitement as the prisoner was dragged, bound with ropes, into the camp.

"Let's burn him as he burned our fields," they said. But just then, God sent His strength to Samson, and he burst the ropes.

"He can't hurt us," shouted the soldiers, "he has no sword." But the next minute they were running for their lives, for Samson had found the jaw bone of an ass, and was killing hundreds of them.

After this, the people of Israel made Samson their leader, and he ruled them for twenty years. He did many brave things, but after a while he began to forget God, and he fell in love with Delilah.

One night, the lords of the Philistines came quietly to her, and said, "Find out what makes Samson strong."

Next time Samson came to visit her, he did not know that there were soldiers hiding in the house. Three times Delilah asked, "Samson, what makes you strong?" Each time he teased her with the wrong answer, until at last tired of her questions, he said, "If you cut off my hair, I shall have broken my vow and God will not help me to be strong any more." Then he went to sleep with his head on Delilah's lap. She beckoned one of the soldiers, and cut off Samson's hair. "The Philistines are upon you, Samson," shouted Delilah, and as the soldiers appeared, Samson sprang at them expecting to knock them over. But all his strength was gone, and the soldiers seized him and, blinding him, dragged him to a terrible prison, where they made him grind corn all day.

The lords of the Philistines were so excited about capturing Samson that they decided to hold a feast at the house of their pretend god, Dagon. Thousands of people came.

"Fetch Samson from the prison," they shouted, "so that we can have some fun." So a boy was sent to fetch Samson, and they made him stand in the middle, between the two pillars that held up the roof.

Poor blind Samson was so weak that he had to hold the pillars for support. Then the Philistines laughed at him, but Samson wanted to serve God as he once had, and beat the Philistine enemies.

His hair had grown long again and he prayed, "O God, give me back my strength, just once more. Let me kill all Your enemies, even if I die with them."

Louder grew the cruel laughter. "Come on, Samson," they jeered, "your God has forgotten you!" Suddenly Samson felt God's strength again, and with one mighty pull he broke the two pillars. With a roar and a crash, the whole roof came toppling down, and the laughter of the Philistines was heard no more.

Judges 15-16:30

A Voice in the Night

It was evening, and all was quiet in the temple when a woman came creeping in. Her name was Hannah. Hiding behind a pillar, she prayed, "O God, please give me a baby. He shall be Yours, I will give him back to You, and he can work for You here in the temple."

Suddenly, she was startled by a voice. It was Eli, the priest, who had come quietly up to her. He did not know she was praying. Hannah told him that she had come to ask God for a special thing.

"Go in peace," he said kindly, "may God answer your prayer." Hannah left the temple feeling happy. God did answer her prayer and she had a baby boy, Samuel.

"Thank You, God," she whispered, as she watched the baby in his cradle, "I give him back to You again."

When Samuel was about four, Hannah took him to the temple.

"I want him to stay here," she said to Eli, "so that he can learn to know God."

Eli was delighted to have Samuel's help, and showed him how to carry out the duties of the temple. Samuel settled down happily. Every year his mother came to see him, bringing with her a new coat for him.

Everybody liked Samuel, except Eli's two sons. They were very wicked men. They worked in the temple with their father, and stole some of the presents people brought for God. God became angry with them, and said to Eli, "I don't want your sons in My house." But Eli would not listen to God. "One day," he thought, "they will look after the people as I do."

One night as Samuel lay asleep, he was awakened by a voice

"Samuel! Samuel!" called the voice again. Up jumped Samuel, and, running once again to Eli, he said, "Here am I, for you did call me."

"No, I did not call," muttered Eli sleepily. Samuel felt a little frightened when he heard the voice once more.

"You *did* call me, Eli," he said, as he reached the old man's bed for the third time.

"Listen, child," Eli said quietly, "it may be that God is speaking to you, and if you hear the voice again, say, 'Speak, Lord, for Your servant is listening.'"

Back ran Samuel with a thumping heart.

"Samuel! Samuel!" came the voice through the darkness, and suddenly Samuel was not frightened any more. The voice was so kind, that he loved God from that very moment.

God gave him a sad message for Eli. Samuel could not sleep. He would have to tell Eli what God had said to him. but he did not want to.

The next morning Eli found him and said, "What did God tell you last night, Samuel?" Miserably, Samuel said, "He said He is angry because you have not stopped your sons doing bad things, and He will not have them as priests to look after the people when you are gone, but they will soon be dead."

This made Eli very sad, for he knew that he had not done as God had asked. Not long after both his sons were killed in battle, and Eli died, too. Samuel became the priest and looked after the people kindly and wisely all his life.

1 Samuel 1:9-3:1-21

calling, "Samuel! Samuel!"

"It must be Eli," he thought, so he ran through the dark, silent temple, until he reached Eli's bed.

"Here I am," he said. Eli opened his eyes.

"Go back to bed," he said, "you were dreaming. I did not call you." Samuel ran back.

The Proud Queen from the South

When Saul was dead, David became king in his place, and what a good king he was! Everyone loved him, and nearly all his people would happily have died for him. He had many sons, and when he was an old man he chose one of them called Solomon to be king after him.

Poor Solomon—how worried he was when he became king!

"I will never be clever enough to rule all these people," he thought, "I feel so young and new to be a king."

That night a strange thing happened. God appeared to him and said, "Solomon, I will give you anything that you want."

"O God," replied Solomon promptly, "please give me wisdom so that I can take care of these people for You."

God was so pleased that the young man had not asked anything for himself, like riches or fame, that He promised to make Solomon the wisest king of all time. "And", He added, "I shall make you rich as well."

Soon the stories of Solomon and his wisdom and riches were being told all over the world, and they reached the ears of the great and proud Queen of Sheba. When she heard them, she was furious. "Surely," she said, "I am the wisest and richest monarch in the world. These stories cannot be true."

She decided she would go and see for herself. "I will ask him such difficult questions that he will never think of the answers," she declared, as she set off at the head of a great line of camels, bearing gold, spices and precious stones. She had to travel over a thousand miles across the hot, dry country of Arabia, but when she reached Solomon's palace she was just as proud as ever. With a rustle of silks and jewels, she swept up the wide marble steps, and it was then that she caught sight of the magnificence of Solomon on his ivory throne and heard the beautiful singing of his many servants, but still she did not believe all the stories.

Solomon was very kind to her, and spent many days entertaining her with food from golden plates. He showed her his ships and golden palaces, and the beautiful temple he had built for God. As she listened to him, gravely and wisely answering every single question that she asked him, at last all her pride was gone, and she said, "I thought the stories that I had heard about you were exaggerated, but now I see that I had not heard even half of all your greatness."

After many happy weeks with the king, she returned to her own country, firmly believing in the God who had made Solomon so wise.

1 Kings 10:1-29

The Man who obeyed God

"We must get rid of Daniel," said the men at their secret meeting. "We do not like the way the king trusts him more than he trusts us." These men had all been given important positions by King Darius, but because Daniel was so wise the king had given him the most important jobs in his whole kingdom. The other ministers of the king didn't like it. They were jealous and angry.

"How can we make the king cross with Daniel?" they kept asking one another. They tried hard to find something against Daniel they could tell the king, but they failed. Daniel was so loyal, faithful and honest that they could not find any fault in him.

Daniel was different from these other men. He was a Jew who worshipped the one true God. Every day he prayed three times to God and always tried to obey God's laws.

One of these evil ministers of the king turned to the others and said, "The only way we can catch Daniel out is through the laws of God." They began to think hard. A wicked smile came over some of their faces

because they were sure they had found a way to get rid of Daniel.

Hurriedly, they went to King Darius. "We believe, O king," they began, "that you should give a command throughout your kingdom that for the next thirty days, no one is allowed to pray to any god or man, but only to the king. If anyone dares to disobey the king's command, he should be thrown into the lions' den."

This suggestion made the king feel very important, so he gave the order and it was proclaimed throughout the kingdom.

The evil men waited. What would Daniel do? They rubbed their hands with glee when they saw Daniel kneel by his open window and pray to his God just as he had always done before. He knew all about the king's command yet he would not stop praying to God. They ran to the king. "O king," they said, "you remember the order you gave that no one had to pray to any god or man, but only to you?"

"I do indeed," replied the king.

"Daniel takes no notice of your command, O king," the men said. "He has disobeyed you. He is still praying to his God three times a day."

On hearing this the king became sad. He liked Daniel very much. All day he tried to find some way to save Daniel. But his wicked ministers reminded him, "King Darius, you know that the laws of our land cannot be changed."

The king was unable to save Daniel. Sadly he gave the order that Daniel was to be thrown into the lions' den. As Daniel was being taken to the den, the king said to him, "I hope that your God will save you."

Daniel 6:1-16